W9-ATG-312

Managing Conflict at Work

Jim Murphy

American Media Publishing
4900 University Avenue
West Des Moines, Iowa 50266-6769
800-262-2557

Managing Conflict at Work

Jim Murphy
Copyright © 1994 by Jim Murphy,
The Business Skills Express Series

Credits:

American Media Publishing:	Art Bauer
	Todd McDonald
	Leigh Lewis
Managing Editor:	Karen Massetti Miller
Editor:	Dave Kirchner
Designer:	Deb Berger
Cover Desgin:	Polly Beaver

Published by American Media Inc.
4900 University Avenue
West Des Moines, IA 50266-6769

Library of Congress Catalog Card Number 94-72157
Murphy, Jim
Managing Conflict at Work

Printed in the United States of America
1997
ISBN 1-884926-25-8

Introduction

As organizations travel further into the future, they face such challenges as expanding market share, improving the quality of service (both internally and externally), building commitment to and consistency in a shared mission, and enhancing individual and team contributions. Meeting these challenges requires managers and associates to constantly initiate and respond to change.

Conflict often goes hand in hand with change. This book will help you to understand and effectively deal with real-life conflict. You will become more aware of the many personal and organizational benefits that are achieved when conflict is viewed as positive rather than negative. Start the book by completing the Self-Assessment. It will highlight the gaps between where you are and where you want to be in your work relationships. This book will give you the support to deal with conflict. Through the use of step-by-step conflict menus, you will be able to manage conflict more thoroughly, objectively, accurately, and quickly.

Whether dealing with a difficult supervisor, associate, customer, or vendor, you will increase your assertiveness and ability to sense, prevent, and resolve conflict. The result will be a better "return on investment" for your organization, and more importantly, for you.

Self-Assessment

This self-assessment will help you to identify gaps, or *conflict,* between what your work environment and relationships are now and what you want them to be.

The first statement of each pair reveals the present state of affairs where you work. The second statement (in italics) reflects what you believe should be the state of affairs at your work in the immediate future. Circle the number that best reflects where on the scale you stand with respect to each statement.

After you select the numbers for each pair of statements, write the difference between those two numbers in the "Difference" column. Do not write a plus or minus sign next to the number. You need only determine the difference. If there is no difference, place a zero in the column.

	None/ Not at All		Moderate Amount/ Sometimes		Large Amount/ Very Often	Difference
1. The amount of respect that my supervisor shows me.	1	2	3	4	5	
The amount of respect that I want my supervisor to show me.	1	2	3	4	5	☐
2. The number of times I sense conflict.	1	2	3	4	5	
The number of times I should sense conflict.	1	2	3	4	5	☐
3. My peers and I discuss how we work together at managing conflict.	1	2	3	4	5	
My peers and I should discuss how we work together at managing conflict.	1	2	3	4	5	☐
4. Quality decisions are reached through the differing views of all employees.	1	2	3	4	5	
Quality decisions should be reached through the differing views of all employees.	1	2	3	4	5	☐

	None/ Not at All		Moderate Amount/ Sometimes		Large Amount/ Very Often	Difference
5. My results reflect my expectations.	1	2	3	4	5	
My results should reflect my expectations.	1	2	3	4	5	☐
6. The authority I have to manage conflict.	1	2	3	4	5	
The authority I should have to manage conflict.	1	2	3	4	5	☐
7. My communications result in common understandings.	1	2	3	4	5	
My communications should result in common understandings.	1	2	3	4	5	☐
8. The number of positive work relationships I have with my peers.	1	2	3	4	5	
The number of positive work relationships I should have with my peers.	1	2	3	4	5	☐
9. The amount of negative conflict that exists with my employees.	1	2	3	4	5	
The amount of negative conflict that should exist with my employees.	1	2	3	4	5	☐
10. The quantity of work I am expected to do.	1	2	3	4	5	
The quantity of work I should be expected to do.	1	2	3	4	5	☐

Turn to the next page for instructions on interpreting your score.

Now take the numbers you have written in the "Difference" column and place them in the blank spaces that correspond with the statement number. Then add the numbers as shown. As you can see, each total corresponds to a specific conflict category of your work environment.

STATEMENT SCORES   **CONFLICT CATEGORY SCORES**

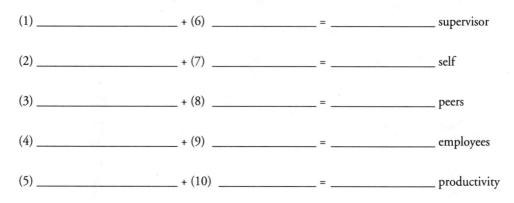

(1) _____ + (6) _____ = _____ supervisor

(2) _____ + (7) _____ = _____ self

(3) _____ + (8) _____ = _____ peers

(4) _____ + (9) _____ = _____ employees

(5) _____ + (10) _____ = _____ productivity

Each category score reflects the degree of conflict that you are, or can be, confronted with. Evaluate in depth the conflict category with the highest score. Then actively use this workbook to understand how to manage your conflicts effectively.

Use the following table to assess your level of conflict:

2 or less   You have no cause for concern.

3   You sense conflict. Although not clearly defined as conflict, unrest is evident. If left unattended, it may grow into a full-blown, damaging conflict.

4   You face conflict. You should identify the cause and develop a strategy to reduce it and your tension.

5 or more   The conflict is explosive. Whether you deal with the conflict or walk away from it, it has escalated to such a point that the basic human rights of people are violated. If continued, it may lead to low self-esteem. Even the winner of this conflict loses.

Table of Contents

Chapter *One*

Conflict: A Part of Life

Chapter Objectives

▶ Recognize protential conflict situations.

▶ Evaluate the benefits of dealing effectively with conflict.

▶ Identify the skills needed to prevent and resolve conflict.

In its simplest terms, conflict is no more than a by-product of growth, change, or innovation. And like change itself, it's practically inevitable. But it's also something that, when handled correctly, can actually promote better communication, guarantee achieving desired results, and improve employee morale and productivity.

> Conflict is no more than a by-product of growth, change, or innovation.

By understanding how to address conflict in a positive results-oriented way, your behavior can set a model for other team members and employees to use in resolving their own conflicts.

This book will give you the tools you need to make that happen!

Recognizing Potential Conflict Situations

Conflict is a daily part of our lives. It can take many forms, from small encounters to full-scale battles. No matter what form a conflict takes, you can learn how to recognize and prevent it. The key to managing conflict is having the courage to take risks and to regularly practice techniques that will give you more control over your environment.

Conflict management techniques enable you to reduce or eliminate those barriers that prevent you from achieving the results desired. When you handle conflict, you not only put out fires but also prevent more from flaring up.

It is probably fair to say that you spend a good part of your day dealing with conflict by solving problems. What do you think of as the first step in solving a problem? If you think as most people do, you probably believe that the first step is identifying the actual problem. But the first step is actually sensing that a problem exists.

No matter what form a conflict takes, you can learn how to recognize and prevent it.

Five Ways to Sense Conflict

The following list provides some key ways to sense conflict on a daily basis:

1. **Be visionary.**
    Visualize how your actions or those of others will cause, or are causing, conflict. Ask yourself *who, what, when, where, how,* and *why* questions to determine potential, as well as present, sources of conflict.

2. **Give feedback.**
    The amount, accuracy, and timeliness of information that you can provide to an individual will help you to understand that person's point of view. Sharing your thoughts and feelings first, in a nonthreatening way, often encourages others to tell you what is on their minds.

3. **Get feedback.**
   Take the time to find out what your associates are thinking and feeling. Do not wait until the last moment to discover that trouble is upon you. Probe for more information by asking questions such as: How so? In what way? Why? and Can you tell me more?

4. **Define expectations.**
   Meet on a weekly basis with your associates to determine priorities for the upcoming week. Any major discrepancies between your expectations will alert you to potential conflict.

5. **Review performance regularly.**
   When supervisors and employees communicate openly about how they are (or are not) working together, they reduce serious conflict and build stronger working relationships.

Risk-Taking and Conflict

In order to manage conflict successfully, you must be willing to take risks. Unfortunately, many people are afraid to take the risk of practicing new techniques. Instead, they seek the secure haven of old, but at times ineffective, behaviors.

In order to manage conflict successfully, you must be willing to take risks.

When you first try to improve your conflict management style, you probably will be somewhat uncomfortable. Do you recall your first interview, the first time you drove a car, or when you first learned to use a computer? After hours of practice, your comfort level no doubt increased, and your performance improved. The same holds true for managing conflict.

1

Take a Moment

If you make a commitment to learn and practice an effective conflict management style, what are the benefits? List all of the benefits to you and to your organization that you think would be gained from managing conflict well.

To you: _____

_____

To your organization: _____

_____

Benefits of Dealing with Conflict

Benefits to You

◆ **Stronger relationships.** You will be able to build stronger relationships as a result of being comfortable expressing your true thoughts and feelings. Fewer mind games will be played, resulting in a less stressful day.

◆ **Increased self-respect.** You will be able to feel good about yourself and will learn not to take criticism personally.

◆ **Personal development and growth.** When you break down some of your own invisible barriers and become more assertive in resolving or preventing conflict, you will learn more and gain support from others.

Benefits to Your Organization

◆ **Improved efficiency and effectiveness.** Employees will be able to do their jobs more efficiently and effectively by focusing their efforts where they will produce the greatest results.

◆ **Creative thinking.** By encouraging people to make, share, and learn from their mistakes, the organization will reap the benefits of creative thinking.

◆ **Synergy, or teamwork.** Managers and associates will be able to focus on serving their customers and each other.

Learning to manage conflict effectively provides a considerable return on your investment.

When you consider the benefits to you and your organization, it becomes clear that learning to manage conflict effectively provides a considerable return on your investment.

Return on Investment for Managing Conflict

No organization can survive without getting a return on its investment. What are some of the returns, or goals, you think your organization wants to achieve? Some of the most common returns relate to sales, profits, productivity, and training.

But what about you and your goals? How would you respond if someone asked you, "Do you work here only to serve this organization and for no other reason?" Unless you are a volunteer, it is a safe bet that your answer would be "Of course not!" What, then, is the return that you are looking for? Since you are using your time and energy to work, what do you want to get in return?

Most people who work for a living state that they work to be successful. No matter what level you have achieved in your career, you eventually will ask yourself, "Do I feel good about what I have done with my life?" In other words, do you feel successful?

Whether intentional or not, *conflict may be your biggest barrier to achieving success.* You should, therefore, commit yourself to mastering an effective conflict management style. You can begin by focusing on a personal goal (your own return on investment) that will motivate you to manage conflict on a constant basis.

Basic Skills to Resolve Conflict

When resolving conflict, many skills and factors can help develop results. The following skills will be useful when resolving conflicts:

> Focus on a personal goal that will motivate you to manage conflict on a constant basis.

Intellectual Skills

- Analytical
- Learning Ability
- Judgment
- Planning
- Organizing
- Perception
- Conceptualizing
- Objectivity
- Flexibility

Emotional Skills

- Honesty
- Persistence
- Ambition
- Self-discipline
- Result-orientation
- Fast pace
- Initiative
- Assertiveness
- Enthusiasm

Interpersonal Skills

- Persuasiveness
- Sensitivity
- Gregariousness
- Listening
- Communication
- Writing

Managerial Skills

- Gives guidance
- Selects competent people
- Motivates
- Terminates/demotes incompetent associates
- Delegates
- Expects professionalism

Take a Moment

As you review the skills previously stated on page 15, identify those skills that you personally feel are well-developed and those that you need to improve upon. This should provide you with a more accurate self-assessment of your development strengths and needs.

Developed skills: _____

_____

_____

_____

_____

Skills needing improvement: _____

_____

_____

_____

_____

Commit yourself to developing and implementing an ongoing plan that will strengthen your conflict management skills.

Commitment

Commit yourself to developing and implementing an ongoing plan that will strengthen your conflict management skills. If you listed several skills that require improvement, choose the skill you feel is a priority, and establish a goal and a time frame for reaching it. In a few months, your newly developed skill will make you more valuable to your organization, and most importantly, to yourself.

Use the Self-Development Plan on the next page as a guide for your development. Share it with your manager for feedback, support, and guidance. Make several copies to use for other skills that you want to improve. If you are a manager, you may want to consider using the plan for an associate whom you are coaching for improved performance.

Self-Development Plan

For: _____   Department: _____

Coach: _____   Target Completion Dates: _____

Development Goal	Strategies to Accomplish the Goal	Results to Be Achieved	Method of Evaluation

By signing the Self-Development Plan, we agree to commit the time and resources necessary to attain the above stated goal.

_____
Associate Signature   *Date*

_____
Supervisor Signature   *Date*

Self-Check: Chapter 1 Review

Answer the questions below. Suggested answers appear on page 78.

1. List five ways to sense conflict.

   a. _____

   b. _____

   c. _____

   d. _____

   e. _____

2. List the four basic skills to resolve conflict.

   a. _____

   b. _____

   c. _____

   d. _____

3. True or False?
   Conflict may be your biggest barrier to achieving success.

4. Conflict is an inevitable product of _____.

5. List the returns on investment you want to achieve from
   your profession.

   _____

   _____

   _____

   _____

6. List the returns on investment your organization wants to
   achieve.

   _____

   _____

   _____

   _____

Chapter *Two*

Conflict: Positive and Negative

Chapter Objectives

▶ Define conflict.

▶ Analyze the positive and negative results of conflict.

▶ Understand the positive and negative flows of conflict.

What does the word *conflict* mean to you? The words given below might come to mind:

- Battle
- Combat
- Rivalry
- Warfare
- Melee
- Run-in
- Clash
- Brawl
- Friction
- Competition
- Struggle
- Collide
- Duel
- Trouble
- Encounter
- Fight

***Conflict* is a set of divergent behaviors, aims, or methods.**

Not really what you would call positive words. But these words represent only a part of a commonly accepted definition of conflict. *Conflict* is a set of divergent behaviors, aims, or methods. After looking at this definition of conflict and the list of words above, you might ask why this chapter describes the negative and positive sides of conflict. What is positive about conflict? Plenty! But before dealing with the positive side of conflict, recall a conflict you have had at work.

Take a Moment

Think of a conflict in which you were involved either at your present organization or a previous one. Answer the following questions:

1. **Who** was involved? List the key people involved in the conflict.

   _____

2. **What** took place? Explain what the actual conflict was about.

   _____

3. **Why** did the conflict occur? Account for as many causes of the conflict as possible.

   _____

4. **Where** did the conflict occur? How did the location affect the conflict?

   _____

5. **When** was the conflict first obvious?

   _____

6. **How** did the conflict affect the organization and the people involved?

   _____

List some of the negative and positive results that came out of the conflict you described.

   _____

   _____

Positive vs. Negative Conflict

You should be able to identify positive and negative results from conflict. Something positive can come out of something that is usually perceived to be negative.

The two definitions given here highlight the differences between negative and positive conflict and how your perception of conflict can lead to positive or negative consequences.

Negative Conflict

In negative conflict, individuals view others as adversaries.

In *negative conflict,* individuals view others as adversaries. They are more concerned about protecting themselves and less, or not at all, concerned about the basic human rights of others. They try to win at all costs and often see people as expenses rather than as investments. They often take negative statements personally and do not try to elicit the true thoughts and feelings of others.

Positive Conflict

In positive conflict, individuals with differing points of view and personalities show mutual respect for each others' thoughts and feelings

In *positive conflict,* individuals with differing points of view and personalities show mutual respect for each others' thoughts and feelings; they consequently develop effective partnerships.

In short, they are supportive of each other. They are secure enough to communicate openly. They avoid playing mind games. Rather than taking negative statements personally, they assert themselves to achieve positive results.

Positive vs. Negative Conflict Case Study

Case
Study

■ Janice Gelnett had been a pediatric nurse for 14 years at a teaching hospital in Chicago. She and her family recently moved to Massachusetts. Janice returned to work a month ago as a pediatric nurse in a small hospital on Cape Cod. Janice has been asked to attend her first monthly staff meeting. In attendance are ten nurses, including Janice; Pat Cleary, who is the director of nursing; and several supervisors and managers, including Janet's nurse-manager, Trisha LoGalbo.

2

Pat:
Unfortunately, we have only a few minutes left for our meeting. Does anyone have questions on what we covered?
(Pat looks around the room quickly and continues on.)

No? Good. Well, since we have a couple of minutes left, let me ask if there are any suggestions about improving our efficiency regarding patient care.

(After a few seconds of silence, Janice is the only one who responds.)

Janice:
Pat, one of the things we did at Chicago was to color-code our charts. I was wondering if that is something you have considered doing here.

Pat:
Well, Janice, as much as I would like to do that, we just can't accomplish the same things that some of the big-city hospitals can afford.

Janice:
It really doesn't have to cost much at all.

Pat:
Trisha, what are your thoughts about this?

Trisha:
That came up before, but it never got off the ground. If a cost analysis is done, we could determine if it would be feasible. Since Janice has worked with this before, maybe she could tell us how it is cost-effective.

Pat:

Well, why don't you two get together and let me know what you find out. OK, anything else?

(There is no immediate response, and the meeting ends.)

Take a Moment

List three clues that identify the negative side of the conflict involving the nurses. Explain why each clue reflects negative conflict.

Clue 1: _____

Why? _____

_____

Clue 2: _____

Why? _____

_____

Clue 3: _____

Why? _____

_____

Debriefing the Case Study—
Three Conflict Clues

Clue 1: The first clue is Pat's unwillingness to answer questions. Remember, one way to sense conflict is to elicit feedback. Conflict could start to build among some of the nurses if they feel that their director does not really want to listen to their opinions.

Clue 2: The second clue is when Pat spoke to Janice, she stated, ". . . we just can't accomplish the same things that some of the big-city hospitals can afford." Pat may have construed Janice's comment as a personal attack. If Pat did misunderstand, conflict may arise.

In addition to not eliciting feedback, Pat is not giving much feedback. When associates share information with their supervisor but receive little in return, they may:

◆ Mistrust their supervisor (and others close to the supervisor).

◆ Fear open communication.

◆ Take fewer risks.

◆ Feel uncertain about their careers.

◆ Lose self-esteem.

> Even if Pat initially is against the change, she should be receptive to listening to any idea that leads to improving the quality of health care.

To strengthen relationships and encourage more suggestions from the other nurses, Pat should share her thoughts with the group about Janice's suggestion. She might say, "Janice, I'm glad you mentioned that. As much as that system may increase our efficiency, I would like to share some of my concerns."

Even if Pat initially is against the change, she should be receptive to listening to any idea that leads to improving the quality of health care.

Clue 3: The third clue points to unclear expectations. Pat ended the meeting by saying, "Well, why don't you two get together and let me know what you find out?" Pat gives no clear direction.

Pat should convey exactly what information she needs and when she needs it: "What I need to know are the pros and cons of establishing this system, the costs involved, and how it will affect the quality of health care. Can you draft a report by next Thursday?"

By explaining expectations of an assignment, future conflict can be prevented or reduced:

◆ There will be few surprises about what should be done.

◆ Less time will be wasted guessing what the boss wants, and more time will be spent on producing effective results.

◆ Relationships will get stronger as associates work closer together to understand each other and what is expected of them.

Positive and Negative Flow of Conflict

The Principle of Positive Conflict

> **Conflict should be viewed and dealt with in an assertive and positive manner.**

Conflict should be viewed and dealt with in an assertive and positive manner. By dealing positively with conflict:

◆ Misunderstandings will be clarified.

◆ Open and ongoing communication will be encouraged.

◆ The ability to sense problems will improve.

◆ Job satisfaction will increase.

The Principle of Negative Conflict

Now consider the effects of not living by the principle of positive conflict:

◆ Individuals grow to distrust each other.

◆ Comments are taken as personal attacks.

◆ The exchange of thoughts, feelings, and information is restricted.

2

Conflict avoidance brings on even more negatives. When managers and associates turn their heads on conflict, they become alienated from each other and from other departments. Because they do not view conflict as positive, they see discussing different points of view as unproductive and a waste of time. Some people avoid conflict because they fear loss of control.

The positive flow of conflict does not guarantee that you always will get what you want. It does emphasize the importance of showing respect for the basic human rights of individuals. Doing so will increase the level of trust between you and your associates as well as increase the likelihood of achieving realistic goals.

Some people avoid conflict because they fear loss of control.

The illustration on page 28 depicts the differences between the positive flow of conflict (the principle of positive conflict) and the negative flow of conflict (conflict avoidance). The negative flow of conflict reflects the thinking that no person or thing should get in your way to achieve your mission or goal. Those who treat people with disrespect may win some battles but rarely will win the war.

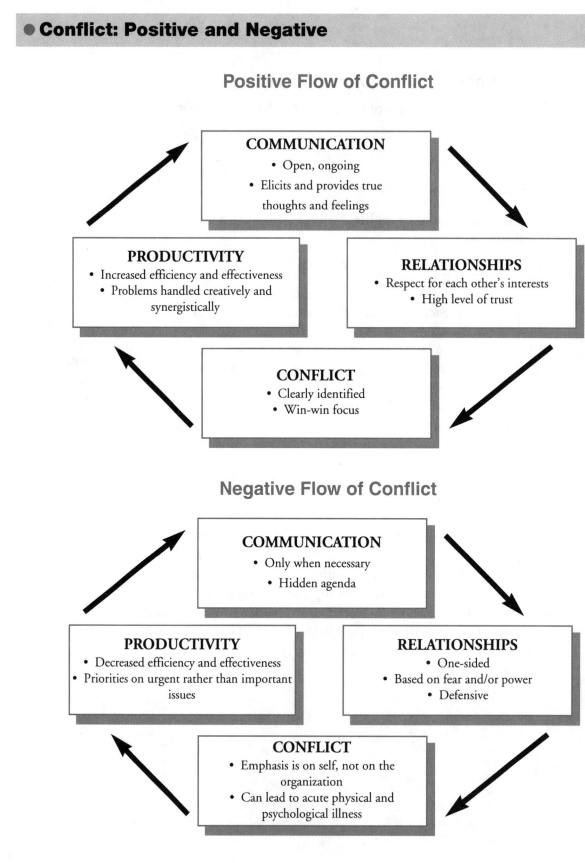

Positive Flow of Conflict

COMMUNICATION
- Open, ongoing
- Elicits and provides true thoughts and feelings

PRODUCTIVITY
- Increased efficiency and effectiveness
- Problems handled creatively and synergistically

RELATIONSHIPS
- Respect for each other's interests
- High level of trust

CONFLICT
- Clearly identified
- Win-win focus

Negative Flow of Conflict

COMMUNICATION
- Only when necessary
- Hidden agenda

PRODUCTIVITY
- Decreased efficiency and effectiveness
- Priorities on urgent rather than important issues

RELATIONSHIPS
- One-sided
- Based on fear and/or power
- Defensive

CONFLICT
- Emphasis is on self, not on the organization
- Can lead to acute physical and psychological illness

Self-Check: Chapter 2 Review

Following each statement below, write a positive response.
Suggested answers for each statement appear on page 78.

Example:
"Excuse me, but I don't agree that implementing that
strategy will increase customer service."
Positive response:
"I'm glad you mentioned that. In what ways do you feel it
would not help?"

2

1. "Boss, I just can't think of any other ways to reduce
absenteeism in our department. I could use any suggestions
you can give me."

   Positive response:

   _____

2. "Why wasn't I invited to the quarterly review meeting?"

   Positive response:

   _____

3. "I'm really getting tired of the boss constantly dumping all
her work on us."

   Positive response:

   _____

Chapter *Three*

What Causes Conflict?

> ## Chapter Objectives
>
> ▶ Develop a system to determine the underlying causes of conflict.
>
> ▶ Learn more about the underlying causes of conflict.
>
> ▶ Learn strategies to achieve goals.

You will be able to manage conflict much more effectively by knowing how the conflict began.

Who or what causes conflict? You probably could generate a long list to answer this question. But no matter how lengthy the list might be, you are the one who must deal with the conflict. You will be able to manage conflict much more effectively by knowing how the conflict began, or if you are sensing conflict, how it may begin.

Finding the Causes of Conflict

For a variety of reasons, many people have difficulty sensing or finding the causes of conflict. Many factors contribute to the difficulty in identifying the correct cause of a conflict:

◆ **Time**
Since time is money, supervisors and associates are encouraged to act quickly.

◆ **Experience**
Some people have gained a vast amount of information and experience over time and believe that their perception is the only one.

◆ **Faith**
Other people blindly, or without question, automatically accept all information as the truth.

◆ **Ego**
Individuals with ego problems have an attitude that states, "I must always show strength by being right the first time." Actually, the opposite is often true of strong managers or associates. Secure individuals with high self-esteem can say to others, and themselves, that they are not certain and need more time or help to come up with an answer.

3

◆ **Poor Training**
Many individuals have not learned how to elicit, observe, and identify human behavior despite the fact that they are trying to influence the behaviors of their boss, staff, peers, and customers.

Many individuals have not learned how to elicit, observe, and identify human behavior.

◆ **Oversensitivity**
Some people believe that if someone wants you to know what happened, or what will happen, he or she will tell you. At times, oversensitive people try to avoid confrontation by not asking for or sharing key information for fear it may offend someone.

Cause of Conflict Menu

Trying to visualize all the possible causes of conflict can become time-consuming and draining. By looking at major categories first, you will be able to focus on the overall cause of conflict. When trying to identify the causes of conflict, it is helpful to think of a menu.

Consider the fact that most restaurants have menus that are broken down into main sections, such as appetizers, salads, entrees, desserts, and so on. Each main section is then broken down into a variety of selections from which to choose. Naturally, menus are organized this way to make it easier for you to select what you like. Imagine how time-consuming and confusing it would be to make a selection if everything being served was on one long list without any order? This concept holds true for conflict.

Recall the definition of conflict from Chapter 2: *Conflict is a set of divergent behaviors, aims, or methods.* Use this to create your own Cause of Conflict Menu. In your menu, you will use three major categories:

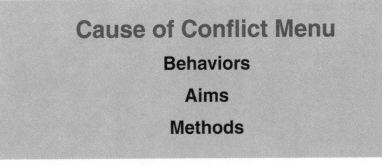

Cause of Conflict Menu

Behaviors

Aims

Methods

Keep in mind the similarities between a restaurant's menu and your Cause of Conflict Menu. The main sections, such as appetizers, salads, and entrees, are replaced by *behaviors, aims,* and *methods.* These three major categories will always be the same. The choices you have under these categories will change depending upon the specific conflict involved.

The following Cause of Conflict Menu is presented as an example of how you might visualize finding the causes of conflict. Each major category is broken down into italicized subsections, and examples are provided under each. Use this menu when trying to identify causes of your own conflicts. As you use it, consistently try to maintain the same order. Doing so will help you remember the seven italicized subsections and increase your ability to see the causes of conflict.

Cause of Conflict Menu

Behaviors

Intellectual
Analytical versus conceptual

Emotional
Assertive versus passive

Interpersonal
Persuasive speaker versus domineering speaker

Managerial
Delegates responsibility and authority versus randomly assigns work

Values (deeply held beliefs that guide behavior)
People viewed as investments versus people viewed as expenses

Aims

Missions, Objectives, Goals, Strategies, Values
Complete by fourth quarter versus complete by third quarter

Methods

Strategies (ways to achieve the aims)
Pay sales representatives on commission versus salary

3

Use this menu when trying to identify causes of your own conflicts.

Take a Moment

Read the conversation between Frank and Bill (below).
Write the causes of conflict under the appropriate sections
of the Cause of Conflict Menu that appears on page 35.
Suggested answers appear on page 80.

Frank:
Bill, maybe one of the reasons Danny isn't performing up to
par is because he hasn't been trained enough to handle the
job.

Bill:
He got the same training everyone else got!

Frank:
I know, but I still want him to get more training. With the
hiring freeze that's on, if you have to let him go, I doubt that
he'll be replaced.

Bill:
All right, since you want it done, I'll have Danny work along
with one of the guys.

Frank:
Good. Let me know how he does.

Bill:

Cause of Conflict Menu

Divergent views of conflict may exist in:

Behaviors

Intellectual

_____

Emotional

_____

Interpersonal

_____

Managerial

_____

Values (deeply held beliefs that guide behavior)

_____

Aims

Missions

_____

Objectives

_____

Goals

_____

Strategies

_____

Values

_____

Methods

Strategies (ways to achieve the aims)

_____

3

Compare your menu with the one on page 80 in the answers section. Do not be overly concerned if you placed a potential conflict cause in the wrong category. Even experienced managers sometimes confuse goals and strategies. The point to remember is that you are learning a systematic way to improve your ability to sense, identify, and resolve conflict.

Even with a menu, you can see that identifying causes is not always simple, especially if you are not getting accurate feedback from others. Complete a Cause of Conflict Menu whenever you need to understand the reason behind any potential or present conflict. It will enable you to be more objective and thorough in your search for the true causes of conflict.

Behaviors That Cause Conflict

Understanding more about human behavior will help you achieve a good return on investment for you and your organization. Your increased comprehension of how people act will have you relying less on gut feelings and more on objective information. We will look at four different behaviors:

♦ Intellectual

♦ Emotional

♦ Interpersonal

♦ Managerial

Intellectual behaviors center on activities relating to the ability to fully understand a situation.

Intellectual Behaviors

Intellectual behaviors center on activities relating to the ability to fully understand a situation, and they are broken down into the following areas:

1. **Analytical**
   Isolates the fundamental parts of a complex problem. Pays attention to details.

2. **Learning ability**
   Can grasp new ideas and concepts.

3. **Judgment**
   Has the mental ability to discern what needs to be done.
   Blends experience and knowledge effectively.

4. **Planning**
   Sets a predetermined course of action.

5. **Organizing**
   Lays out tasks in a logical sequence. Establishes and
   maintains priorities.

6. **Perception**
   Observes the details and overall scope of situations and
   problems.

7. **Conceptualizing**
   Has the ability to form mental concepts and see the overall
   picture.

8. **Objectivity**
   Separates fact from feeling when appraising ideas.

9. **Flexibility**
   Can change a course of action when new information makes
   it apparent that another way would be more effective.

By understanding how people involved in your conflict will
react due to their intellectual behavior, you can determine
appropriate actions to take.

3

Emotional Behaviors

Because conflict is such an emotional issue, you will find that this behavior area outweighs all others combined. Part of solving conflict is dealing with the real problem. But you must often deal first with emotions, such as:

> **You must often deal first with emotions before you can resolve a conflict.**

1. **Honesty**
   Acts sincerely and candidly. Avoids deception or playing games.

2. **Persistence**
   Pursues aims despite barriers and disappointing occurrences.

3. **Ambition**
   Shows a strong desire to reach personal goals.

4. **Self-discipline**
   Deals with difficult or unrewarding assignments without procrastinating.

5. **Results orientation**
   Determined to achieve meaningful results. Concentrates on preventing and solving problems to reach stated goals.

6. **Fast pace**
   Accomplishes work expeditiously. Consistently shows a strong sense of urgency.

7. **Initiative**
   Starts work independently, especially without direction or in an unstructured setting.

8. **Assertiveness**
   Able to express honest thoughts and feelings to others while treating them with respect. Shows strong self-esteem.

9. **Enthusiasm**
   Constantly expresses a positive attitude. Accents the positive side of situations while recognizing the negative.

When managing conflict, remember the importance of managing emotions, as well.

Interpersonal Behaviors

Interpersonal behavior deals with how people relate to others involved in the conflict. Some of the characteristics are:

1. **Persuasiveness**
   Influences the thinking of others. Overcomes objections to sell ideas.

2. **Sensitivity**
   Shows appreciation for and understanding of others. Anticipates how others will feel as a result of what is said or done.

3. **Gregariousness**
   Expresses a personal interest in people. Is sociable as well as easy and enjoyable to speak with.

4. **Listening**
   Takes the responsibility to listen to people, without judgment, by inviting the conversation to continue.

5. **Communication**
   Establishes common understandings. Transfers thoughts and feelings with clarity. Articulates.

6. **Writing**
   Communicates clearly in writing.

Appropriate interpersonal behavior is crucial to managing conflict in a positive manner.

Interpersonal behavior **deals with how people relate to others involved in the conflict.**

3

Managerial Behaviors

Don't let the word *managerial* fool you. You don't have to be a manager to manage. You may be in a team or peer situation where the following characteristics will be in great demand:

1. **Selects competent people.**
    Assesses people's strengths and weaknesses.

2. **Gives guidance.**
    Lets associates know what is expected of them and suggests an appropriate direction for their development. Coaches and trains associates.

3. **Motivates.**
    Knows the personal goals of associates and helps them to achieve those goals when they perform competently.

4. **Delegates.**
    Assigns work based on associates' knowledge, skills, and needs. Shares responsibility and authority.

5. **Expects professionalism.**
    Encourages excellence by communicating high-performance standards. Empowers people to be committed, competent, and consistent in the performance of their jobs.

6. **Terminates or demotes incompetent associates.**
    Decides objectively, or influences those who do decide, to transfer, demote, or fire nonperforming associates.

You can have incredible influence over others and how they deal with conflict if you model the correct managerial behaviors.

You can have incredible influence over others and how they deal with conflict if you model the correct managerial behaviors.

Values

As described in the Cause of Conflict Menu, *values* are strongly held principles that guide an individual's or organization's behavior. Wherever disparity appears about basic values, conflict will explode.

3

Take a Moment

The exercise below will help you to evaluate the compatibility of your values and an associate's values. As soon as any dissimilarity is determined, you will have three important choices to make. Decide whether to accept, change, or leave the environment (not necessarily your organization). Having to endure the values of someone who opposes your rooted beliefs, just for job security, often leads to poor performance, and worse, low self-esteem. No one wins in this conflict.

Next to each value below, check **Agree** or **Disagree.** If you disagree, plan an action that you, and possibly others, can take to prevent, reduce, or resolve any negative conflict based on your differences.

Value	My Associate and I	
	Agree	Disagree
1. Everyone has basic human rights and should be treated with respect.	_____	_____
2. People should be able to communicate their honest thoughts and feelings.	_____	_____
3. Success of any organization is based on working effectively as a team.	_____	_____
4. In order to improve total quality, everyone should be open to change.	_____	_____

Take a Moment *(continued)*

Value	My Associate and I Agree	Disagree
5. Having a sense of urgency is a major condition for success.	_____	_____
6. Having a sense of humor is a major condition for success.	_____	_____
7. Individuals should be empowered with the necessary authority to accomplish their work.	_____	_____
8. All individuals should be appreciated for the work they do.	_____	_____
9. The opportunity for promotion and growth should always exist.	_____	_____
10. Achieving success should be planned on a short-term as well as a long-term basis.	_____	_____

List two of your own values and then check whether you and your associate agree or disagree with them.

11. _____

12. _____

Even if you checked only one value difference in the exercise on pages 41 and 42, you should develop a detailed plan similar to the one described on page 21. Answer the *who, what, why, where, when,* and *how* questions as they apply to this difference.

If you noted more than one value difference in the exercise on pages 41 and 42, concentrate on the one value that:

◆ Is most important to you.

◆ Seems to be the underlying cause of many conflicts.

◆ Will produce a significant benefit for you and your organization.

3

The Aims Hierarchy

Aims relate to expected outcomes and the roles that managers and associates assume in order to achieve them. Many successful organizations, from small businesses to conglomerates, follow a system that defines their long- and short-term expectations, or aims. Such a system is called *strategic planning.* It consists of clearly defining the organization's mission, objectives, goals, strategies, and values. If any part of the strategic plan is misunderstood, negative conflict will result. The following pyramid depicts the hierarchy of these items:

> *Aims* relate to expected outcomes and the roles that managers and associates assume in order to achieve them.

♦ **Mission**
The reason that an organization exists.

♦ **Objectives**
Broad statements of a desired future condition based on what the organization wants to achieve.

♦ **Goals**
Statements of specific, measurable results to be achieved in accomplishing the objectives.

♦ **Strategies**
Descriptions of specific tasks required to accomplish the goals.

♦ **Values**
The foundation of an organization; a deeply held set of beliefs that guides organizational behavior.

Mission

If a new employee approached you and asked, "Why does our organization—or department—exist?" what would you say? Would you have a response?

Never develop a mission if it is just going to sit around and gather dust.

Unfortunately, many businesses do not have mission statements. Or there may be a mission, but no one makes it come alive. Never develop a mission if it is just going to sit around and gather dust. A mission is meant to strengthen managers and their associates by promoting pride and a common understanding about their direction, priorities, and roles. Review the mission statements on the next page. Do they convey a clear picture of why these businesses exist?

Sample Mission Statements

> To remain a leading, profitable, human resource development firm that is actively dedicated to improving individuals' knowledge, skills, and attitudes so they can be better motivated and prepared to reach or surpass organizational and personal goals.

3

> The Listening Center is strongly committed to providing an enthusiastic, ethical, and caring work environment where associates are given the opportunity to fulfill their potential and sustain the highest possible level of service and value to our clients.

Do You Know Your Organization's Mission?

If you do not know what your organization's mission is, respectfully ask about it. Rather than inquiring during a meeting, where your supervisor may be uncomfortable or defensive, discuss it privately. If a mission has not been formed, try to convince your manager of the benefits of developing one.

Depending upon your boss and yourself, there may be some uneasiness during such a discussion, especially if this subject has never been brought up before. Therefore, use one of the basic skills needed to resolve or prevent conflict persuasiveness.

If you do not know what your organization's mission is, respectfully ask about it.

Before the meeting, visualize what your supervisor may say and how you will respond. Convince your supervisor that doing something different, such as putting together a mission, will add to the good things that have already been accomplished. It will also reduce any negative conflict since only issues that relate to the mission would be dealt with. When you feel it is appropriate, use humor to reduce any tension. Prevent your supervisor from feeling that change is a sign that there is a major problem in the organization. That is not the message you're trying to get across.

Objectives and Goals

Objectives and goals will vary from one organization to another. They can relate to many outcomes, such as:

◆ Safety	◆ Total quality	◆ Grievances
◆ Quality assurance	◆ Quantity	◆ Damages
◆ Sales	◆ Payroll costs	◆ Employee turnover
◆ Inventory levels	◆ Loss prevention	◆ Transportation costs

To be valid, goals must be *specific, measurable,* and must *answer* the following three questions:

◆ **Who** will accomplish the goal?

◆ **What** is to be achieved? In other words, how will anyone know the goal was achieved?

◆ **When** will the goal be accomplished?

Take a Moment

Answer the questions that follow each goal. Answers appear on page 78.

1. "Pat Garmella will conduct acceptable orientations for all new employees in her department by the first six months of this year."

   Is this a valid goal? Why or why not?

   _____

   _____

   _____

   _____

2. "Bob Weldon will reduce delinquent accounts by three percent in his department by year-end."

   Is this a valid goal? Why or why not?

   _____

   _____

   _____

   _____

3

Strategies and Values

There are many strategies to achieve goals. When setting goals and objectives, you will get more:

◆ Ownership

◆ Participation

◆ Creativity

. . . when strategies can be developed by those responsible for achieving the outcomes.

Much time, money, frustration, and inefficiency can be expended when the cause of conflict is misidentified. Take the time to determine the real or potential reason for conflict by using the Cause of Conflict Menu. By applying it regularly, you will build your confidence to understand who or what created the conflict.

Once you sense or know the creator of conflict, you are more likely to prevent or resolve it effectively and boost your credibility in the process.

Methods for Achieving Aims

We have talked in-depth about the first two categories on our Cause of Conflict Menu. Now let's spend time on the third category—methods.

The way we do things offers potential causes of conflict just like our personal behaviors. In some cases, people just rub us the wrong way, therefore causing conflict. Sometimes the way people carry out their duties—their methods—rub us wrong as well.

Think about some of the people you work with. Does the way they complete their job responsibilities rub you the wrong way? Why?

By understanding your own work style and the work styles of others, you are taking the first step in understanding how people's methods can cause conflict.

Self-Check: Chapter 3 Review

Answer the questions listed below. Suggested answers appear on page 79.

1. True or False?
    Many factors contribute to the difficulty in identifying the correct cause of a conflict.

2. True or False?
    Many people sense or find the cause of conflict immediately.

3. True or False?
    Even experienced managers sometimes confuse goals and strategies.

4. True or False?
    Completing a Cause of Conflict Menu will enable you to be more objective and thorough in your search for the true causes of conflict.

5. True or False?
    Setting goals, strategies, and standards rarely reduces conflict.

6. The definition of conflict is a set of _____, _____, and _____.

7. The four behaviors that cause conflict are _____, _____, _____, and _____.

8. To be valid, goals must include answers to three questions:

    _____

    _____

    _____

Chapter *Four*

Resolving Conflict

Chapter Objectives

▶ Identify the actions needed to resolve conflict.

▶ Learn five steps to successful conflict management.

Whether you're a manager dealing with conflict in your department or an individual faced with conflict in your team or work group, the techniques for conflict management described in this chapter can help you approach conflict in a positive manner. But before we begin, a piece of advice: If you are reading this chapter first because you want a quick solution to a problem that is causing negative conflict, think again. Effectively resolving and preventing conflict is an ongoing process. Reading and practicing the material covered in the previous chapters of this book will help you develop a more intelligent, thorough, and objective approach to managing conflict positively.

If you are reading this chapter first because you want a quick solution to a problem that is causing negative conflict, think again.

The Five Steps to Successful Conflict Management

To effectively deal with conflict situations in both your business and personal life, follow these five easy steps for successful conflict management:

- Step 1: Take responsibility for dealing with conflict.

- Step 2: Uncover, define, and discuss the real problem.

- Step 3: Ask questions and listen!

- Step 4: Set goals and create an action plan.

- Step 5: Follow up.

Step 1: Take Responsibility for Dealing with Conflict

It's part of human nature to want to avoid conflict. Unpleasant and often emotional confrontations naturally make us feel uncomfortable. That's why when we sense or perhaps even directly observe a conflict among our employees or team members, we sometimes "stick our heads in the sand," hoping that the problem will work itself out (or even more unrealistically, that one of the players may even quit or transfer to a different position).

None of this is too surprising. We probably were taught from the time we were children not to get involved in conflicts. Perhaps we even experienced a situation in which intervening in a conflict actually appeared to make matters worse.

If this is indeed the case, it's time to leave that training and those experiences behind. The fact is, taking the initiative to intervene in a conflict situation has much greater potential for making matters better—for turning what may have looked like a hopeless lose-lose predicament into a win-win opportunity.

4

Intervening in a conflict situation has greater potential for making matters better than ignoring the problem or hoping it will go away.

"You Can't Win If You Don't Play"

You may have heard this old saying before. And in its simple truth is buried the first step to successful conflict management: You can't turn a conflict into a *win-win opportunity* unless you first make the decision to take personal responsibility for dealing with the conflict.

> You can't turn a conflict into a *win-win opportunity* unless you first make the decision to take personal responsibility for dealing with the conflict.

Since you're reading this book, you've probably already made that decision. If so, congratulations, because it's often the single hardest part of the conflict-management process.

The bottom line is that you, and the people in your department and on your management teams, need no longer view conflict as totally "negative" or as an obstacle to be avoided, or worse, ignored. You need not look at intervening and managing conflict as the corporate equivalent of pulling teeth. With the proper tools and advice, you'll gain the confidence you need to deal positively and assertively with conflict. You'll not only prevent many instances of potential conflict from ever developing in the first place, but you'll actually learn how to turn existing conflicts into opportunities for growth and improved interpersonal relationships.

And consider this bonus: The energy you used to spend worrying about the conflict—about what your people are really thinking, about loss of productivity, and about when and if the conflict will ever resolve itself—you'll begin to use constructively and productively to confront the situation head-on and work toward its solution.

Step 2: Uncover, Define, and Discuss the Real Problem

Uncover the Real Problem

Is there any mistake worse than sensing or observing a developing conflict and then failing to act and take responsibility for it? You bet there is! It's taking responsibility and acting with incomplete or inaccurate information about the true nature of the problem.

Not only does that waste your time as you work to resolve something that's not at the heart of the real conflict, it leaves the real problem unchecked and can further lower morale if others sense that your "solution" isn't really effective.

Define the Conflict

"But that's an easy mistake to avoid," you might say. "I would never take any kind of action to resolve a conflict unless the source of the problem was crystal clear to me."

The fact is, when the source of your problem appears "crystal clear," that's often a red flag to stop for a moment and challenge your first impression, strong as it may be. Sometimes you can bring preconceived notions to the problem that you're not consciously aware of. Other times, and for a variety of reasons, associates may be reluctant to speak up and share information that would shed new light on the real problem.

Cast yourself in the role of a detective who needs to check, double-check, and triple-check every shred of evidence. Your task at this point isn't to implement any kind of solution. Step back and forget for a moment even trying to solve the problem. Instead, your task is simply to uncover and accurately define the problem.

> Cast yourself in the role of a detective who needs to check, double-check, and triple-check every shred of evidence.

4

Discussing the Problem

It's been proven that the surest, most efficient way to ferret out the real source of a problem is to bring together all of the people involved for an open and frank discussion. Although it's possible to meet individually with each of the people involved to get the information you need, you may run the risk of appearing to place blame on an individual in a one-on-one meeting.

And there's also the possibility that you'll have to schedule two or even three meetings with one or more employees as you follow up on new information you've been given.

Of course, there will be situations in which the conflict involves weighty issues of employment, legality, or sexual harassment when it's unwise to hold a group meeting. Anytime you're unsure which way to proceed, you should seek advice from your manager or your company's human resources personnel.

> **The surest way to discover the real source of a problem is to bring those involved together for a discussion.**

But even aside from those special instances, there are bound to be times when you'll be tempted to disregard this advice and meet with the people involved one at a time. If the conflict involves strong personalities, you may feel you'd be lighting a powder keg to bring them all together in the same room.

Then, too, you may simply feel awkward or uncomfortable in what could develop into a heated and emotional discussion. The path of least resistance, you may reason, is to do all you can to keep emotion out of your discussions.

Don't Keep Emotion Out of the Discussion—
Let It Out!

Even though at times emotions may run high during your meeting, getting them out on the table and acknowledging them is an important part of moving ahead and resolving the conflict.

If you don't let people vent their emotions and give everyone present the opportunity to acknowledge them, those powerful emotions will just continue to percolate under the surface. And inevitably, they will undercut any progress you seem to be making toward a permanent and positive resolution to the conflict. The bottom line is: Until you get the emotions out of the way, you simply won't be able to focus on the real problem and work toward a solution.

But don't worry. Expressing true emotions doesn't mean that your meeting needs to become a shouting match. There are ways to promote totally open communication—with no holding back—and to do it in a controlled and productive way. You just have to establish the ground rules.

The Four Ground Rules: Your Keys to
Conducting Controlled, Productive Meetings

Here they are: Four simple ground rules that, if followed, will lead you systematically to the true source of the conflict. The information you receive using these rules may indeed confirm your initial impression of the problem you need to solve. Or it may surprise you and point you in a totally new direction.

But one thing is for sure: These ground rules will set the stage to discuss true emotions—all in a way that promotes sharing, trust, and a commitment to work toward a common goal.

> **Until you get the emotions out of the way, you simply won't be able to focus on the real problem and work toward a solution.**

4

It's good to state these ground rules at the start of your meeting and to explain a bit about what each one really means as you go along. Then ask if anyone has any questions about the rules and if everyone is in agreement to abide by them.

Reassure those involved in your conflict that your purpose in meeting isn't to find fault or place blame but just to get the real source of the problem out on the table so everyone can work together effectively to solve it.

State these ground rules at the start of your meeting.

◆ **Ground Rule 1: Everyone will be open and honest.**
Because your sole purpose is the discovery of any and all information that helps define the problem at the heart of the conflict, this ground rule is key. You'll want to do all you can to create an atmosphere of trust, and yes, even to allow for the venting of emotions.

◆ **Ground Rule 2: Everyone will have a say and be heard.**
Assuring everyone that they will have an equal opportunity to be heard—and all in front of the others—will underscore that you sincerely want to understand and solve the conflict fairly and objectively.

This is where the advantages of holding one group meeting, with all participants present, really come into play. Everyone can see that each person's contributions and opinions are equally valued and considered—that there's no favoritism. And everyone will have the opportunity to hear and react to all that is said.

◆ **Ground Rule 3: Everyone will listen to each other without argument or negative reaction and will keep a positive, caring attitude.**
It's your job to make sure that nothing occurs in the meeting to impede or interrupt each person's explanations and answers. You can expect the occasional emotional outburst or objection.

But even though emotions do have a place in your discussion, during "someone else's say" isn't it. Don't hesitate to remind the person who interrupts that he or she agreed to listen objectively and without argument until each person has finished.

And don't overlook body language, either. A derisive roll of the eyes or exhalation of breath can send the same message as an outright verbal interruption. If you observe this kind of inappropriate body language, it's your responsibility, once again, to remind the person that he or she is not abiding by the agreed-upon ground rules and ask for everyone's cooperation.

Sometimes people's opinions and feelings are so strongly held that, when they express them, they come out as emotionally charged criticisms.

◆ **Ground Rule 4: Opinions and feelings must be supported by facts or examples of specific behavior.** Again, sometimes peoples' opinions and feelings are so strongly held that, when they express them, they come out as emotionally charged criticisms. But that's okay—as long as the person maintains a caring attitude and does not personally attack someone else, and as long as he or she is able to support his or her opinions with facts and examples of behavior.

4

That's the only way to ensure that the information you get is accurate, unbiased, and specific—the only kind that will help you define and resolve the conflict.

Step 3: Ask Questions and Listen!

If you've already followed the first two steps to successful conflict management, congratulations! The hardest work is behind you. You took the first major plunge and accepted responsibility for dealing with the conflict head-on. And, before you attempted to implement a solution, you decided to meet with all of the people involved to make sure you understood the real problem.

You explained to everyone why it's important to follow the four meeting ground rules as you all work toward your common goal. All of your ground work is in place. Now there are just two things you need to do to realize the maximum benefit from your meeting: *Ask questions and listen!*

> There are just two things you need to do to realize the maximum benefit from your meeting: *Ask questions and listen!*

That sounds simple, and basically it is. Still, there are valuable tips you should know about that will help you ask questions and listen to answers like a pro, and that will maximize your return on the time you invest in the meeting. When you follow these tips, you'll also send the message that you're sincerely interested in what people have to say.

How to Ask Questions Like a Pro

You've heard the expression "garbage in, garbage out," which is basically just another way of saying that the quality of your output is no better than the quality of your input. Well, the same relationship applies to questions and answers. To get the right answers, you have to ask the right questions.

> To get the right answers, you have to ask the right questions.

◆ **Try to avoid asking** *closed-ended questions*—questions that could be answered with a simple "yes" or "no." Instead, ask *open-ended* questions that prompt thoughtful, informative answers.

  Rather than asking, "Was the shipping department backlog a problem for your work group?" ask, "What exactly happened in your work group as a result of the backlog in the shipping department?"

◆ **Choose your words carefully so they're a true reflection of the kind of response you're looking for.** In the example above, note the use of the word "exactly." That word acts as a signal that what's appropriate in this instance is a detailed response, perhaps complete with illustrative examples. Other words and phrases you'll find helpful are "specifically" and "can you give me an example . . . ."

◆ **Follow up with targeted** *probing questions* **if an initial answer misses the mark or doesn't go into as much detail as you'd like.** Questions such as, "Why do you say that?" "What do you think caused that result?" and "Is there one example of this kind of miscommunication that comes to mind?" often will amplify and clarify the initial response. Then indicate your appreciation and understanding of the additional information you've received by nodding your head or by paraphrasing what was said when you respond.

4

♦ **Finally, learn what to do when someone simply refuses to talk.** Often, people who rarely hesitate to complain are the ones least likely to open up in front of their supervisors. Sometimes, they're also the ones who could really contribute useful information or suggestions, and one of your goals is to ask questions from all angles and sides of the problem. Often, you can put these people at ease by asking candidly for their advice: "What would you like to see happen in this particular situation that just isn't happening now?" That one question lets the person know that you're interested in his or her recommendations and input and usually will prompt a helpful response.

Listen Actively and Objectively

If you used to think of listening as a passive type of activity, think again! Actually, think of one or two people with whom you've consistently felt comfortable talking in an open and candid way.

Try to remember how they reacted as you spoke. Chances are, they were anything but passive. In fact, they may have seemed to hang onto your every word, nodding frequently to give encouraging feedback as you spoke, and following up with statements or questions that proved they understood and were interested in what you just said. These folks no doubt realized that successful listening is very much an active endeavor, and they probably put these tips into practice:

♦ **Listen objectively and with an open mind.** Try to be aware of any expectations or preconceived ideas you may have regarding what you're about to hear and put them aside. Evaluate what you hear as if it's being written on a clean slate.

60

◆ **Reassure the other person that you're interested in his or her perception of the situation.** There are lots of ways to do this. One of the simplest and most effective is just to nod your head when key points are made. Another is to jot down occasional notes—but don't do it at the expense of losing valuable eye contact with the person who's talking to you.

◆ **Offer positive feedback by paraphrasing what you've heard and following up with questions based on the new information.** A simple "Let me see if I understand . . ." followed by "Did I get that right?" immediately tells the other person that you've been paying careful attention. And if by chance there is a discrepancy in your playback of the information, you'll get the needed clarification right on the spot.

Wonderful things can happen when you show people that you're listening actively and objectively. Your feedback tells them that you understand and are sympathetic to their problems. And when that happens, you'll find that they, like you, will begin to take a personal responsibility for working toward a solution to the problem!

Step 4: Set Goals and Create an Action Plan

As we said, one of the benefits of taking the time to ask effective questions and actively listen to their answers is that people will respond by volunteering their own possible solutions to the problem.

When they do . . . *listen to them!*

4

When people volunteer possible solutions to a problem, listen to them.

Getting Commitment

People naturally are reluctant to work toward a problem's solution until they honestly "buy into it." It's a fact that the people who are closest to the problem also are the ones most likely to come up with a practical, workable solution.

Be alert when an associate in your meeting offers a suggestion for regular update meetings with team members, or perhaps the initiation of a new form or report that includes information key people need to have. That person may have just handed you the action plan you need to solve the conflict problem!

When setting goals, remember that they must be specific, measurable, and attainable. Ask thoses involved in the conflict to help determine goals and generate a plan for meeting them in order to gain commitment and ensure understanding.

Communication Is Key

Improve the frequency and clarity of your interdepartmental communication.

Note that the common thread in the two possible action plans just mentioned is improved communication. People naturally have a tendency to assume that others think just as they do. And although successful action plans usually focus on ways to change behaviors or procedures, they almost always also involve strategies for improving communication.

Need we state the obvious? If you would like to do just one thing on a daily basis that would have maximum impact on avoiding potential conflicts and increasing employee morale, improve the frequency and clarity of your interdepartmental communication.

Finally, don't let the meeting end until you've found out if its communication has been successful. Ask if everyone is in agreement on the problem that has been defined. Find out if all believe that the action plan you've discussed is the right one. Don't make the mistake of railroading through an action plan that some or all of the people believe in only halfheartedly. Ask for everyone's honest commitment. And if you sense that it's not entirely there, open up the meeting to more discussion.

> **Finally, don't let the meeting end until you've found out if its communication has been successful.**

Step 5: Follow Up

At this point in the conflict management cycle, you may feel as if you've done it all. You've taken personal responsibility for dealing with the conflict. You've held meetings to discuss and define the real problem where you asked the right questions and actively listened to what the people told you. Then, together, you decided on—and committed to—the goals and the action plan that will work toward them. What could possibly be left to do?

To answer that question, think for a moment about all of the possible obstacles you could encounter as you try to implement that action plan. First and maybe the most obvious, you may not be able to recall the specific details of the action plan that you agreed upon. Then too, with time, the enthusiasm and camaraderie that was generated in your initial meeting may fade a bit, giving a potential foothold to some of the feelings and behaviors that may have caused the initial conflict.

4

By anticipating obstacles like these, you can help ensure the eventual success of your efforts. But in order to do that, you need to decide on and implement the appropriate follow-up procedures.

Follow-Up Actions

1. Before you conclude your meeting, tell your associates that you'd like to summarize your understanding of what you've accomplished in writing, and then agree on a date and time for a follow-up meeting.

2. Within a day or two of your meeting, send a note thanking participants for their input and summarizing the steps of the action plan you've agreed to, as you understand them. Be specific here. If there are responsibilities assigned, reiterate them and include the agreed-upon dates by which they'll be accomplished. Invite feedback. Tell them that you don't view your meeting together as "the end of the road" but as the beginning of a new, positive, concerted group effort toward your common goal. And because you realize that open communication is the key to resolving—and avoiding— conflict in the first place, make sure everyone understands that your door is always open.

> **Make sure everyone understands that your door is always open.**

3. Finally, include the date, time, and place of your first follow- up meeting together.

There. You really have done it all! And the responsibility, assertiveness, and sincerity you've shown throughout this conflict management process is about to reward you and your company with improved communication, morale, and productivity.

Self-Check: Chapter 4 Review

Answer the following questions. Answers appear on page 79.

1. List the five steps to successful conflict management.

   a. _____

   b. _____

   c. _____

   d. _____

   e. _____

4

2. List the three tips used when listening actively and objectively.

   a. _____

   b. _____

   c. _____

3. List the four ground rules that, if followed, will lead you to the true source of the conflict.

   a. _____

   b. _____

   c. _____

   d. _____

Chapter *Five*

Dealing with Conflict Assertively

Chapter Objectives

▶ Identify assertiveness.

▶ Identify barriers to assertiveness.

▶ Develop an assertiveness goal.

▶ Strengthen your basic human rights.

▶ Learn ways to think and act more assertively.

Picture yourself sitting at a table with other people during a wedding reception. One of your favorite songs is being played and you feel an overpowering urge to rush onto the dance floor. So you ask your date:

You:
This is a great song. Do you want to dance?

Your date:
No, thanks.

You:
Why not?

Your date:
I'd really like to, but there's no one else on the dance floor, and I don't want to be the first one out there.

You:
Come on, by the time we get out there, there will be other people dancing!

Your date:
Sorry.

Does this seem familiar? What are your thoughts about how your date is acting? The results you achieve from actively using this book will depend upon the assertiveness you show to be "the first one on the dance floor."

Rather than consistently waiting for others to start resolving conflict their way, an assertive person puts control of the future into his or her own hands, not someone else's.

You are your own boss. People will know that by the way you teach them to treat you.

What Is Assertiveness?

Rarely will you be able to bring out the best in others and yourself unless you treat conflict, as well as your life, assertively. The way you influence others on a daily basis often affects the amount of conflict that will come your way.

Therefore, it is critically important to make assertiveness an intimate part of your life.

In addition to stronger relationships, increased self-respect, and personal development and growth, you will get the following benefits from being assertive:

5

Rarely will you be able to bring out the best in others and yourself unless you treat conflict, as well as your life, assertively.

◆ Increased confidence to express how you really think and feel.

◆ Ability to say "no" respectfully.

◆ A more proactive approach to sensing problems.

◆ Improved communication skills to elicit common understandings.

◆ Encouragement for others to be assertive.

- ◆ Expectations clarified. Bringing out the best of your abilities, some of which you may not yet know you have.

- ◆ Better ability to deal with stress at work and at home.

- ◆ Feeling of more control over your surroundings.

- ◆ Reduced or eliminated prejudices and stereotypes.

Barriers to Assertiveness

Many managers and associates face numerous barriers that prevent them from becoming more assertive and achieving all of the preceding rewards. Are you aware of any that you face?

Take a Moment

Each statement here represents a barrier to assertiveness. Circle the number that indicates how important each barrier is in preventing you from being more assertive in dealing with situations and conflict.

The Effect It Has on Your Assertiveness

Barrier	Little		Moderate		Large
1. I am unable to say no to requests.	1	2	3	4	5
2. I find it difficult to work with superiors or those in authority.	1	2	3	4	5
3. I feel uneasy asking others to do things.	1	2	3	4	5
4. I feel uncomfortable admitting mistakes.	1	2	3	4	5
5. I have difficulty probing people to find out how they really think and feel.	1	2	3	4	5
6. I have difficulty expressing my own true thoughts and emotions.	1	2	3	4	5
7. I get manipulated into doing things I do not want to do.	1	2	3	4	5
8. I get uptight when I receive negative criticism.	1	2	3	4	5
9. I have difficulty initiating and building relationships with people at work.	1	2	3	4	5

5

After assessing which barrier prevents you the most from being more assertive, develop a written goal and strategy that will guide you to reduce or eliminate the barrier. Use the form on page 70 to develop your assertiveness goals.

Assertiveness Goal

Name: _____   Date Goal Written: _____

Department: _____   Evaluation Dates: _____

Goal to Be Achieved	Strategies (Tasks Required to Accomplish the Goal)
	1.
	2.
	3.
	4.

Assert Your Basic Human Rights

Basic human rights are meant for everyone. Basic rights allow all individuals to be treated with respect. They include the right to:

◆ Say no without feeling guilty.

◆ Express your true thoughts and feelings.

◆ Have more control over your position.

◆ Feel good about yourself.

Expressing your true thoughts and feelings by differing with your supervisor may pose several risks. You may be excluded from a promotion, a higher pay increase, or some meetings.

If you choose to allow your basic human rights to be violated, you may still bring home a paycheck but not much self-respect. It's back to the three choices you have. Accept being treated disrespectfully, change the way you are treated, or leave your department or organization.

Basic human rights allow all individuals to be treated with respect.

5

Assertiveness vs. Passiveness and Aggressiveness

Passive and aggressive behaviors (as well as assertive behavior) also influence others. All three behaviors have one thing in common—basic human rights. If you choose to maintain or further achieve your basic human rights, then being assertive, rather than passive or aggressive, will prove to be your best strategy.

Assertive People

Assertive people personify strong self-esteem.

Assertive people personify strong self-esteem. They are risk takers and normally even-tempered. They will not allow someone else to control their future. Many assertive people were once passive or aggressive.

Passive People

Passive people accept others' thoughts and feelings without objection or resistance.

Passive people accept others' thoughts and feelings without objection or resistance. They may show little or no respect for their own basic human rights. Passive people lack confidence in themselves. In many cases, they do not feel competent about their own abilities. They do not feel liked by others or even themselves. They are stagnant.

Aggressive People

Aggressive people show little or no respect for others' basic human rights.

This is a behavior that reflects hostile attitudes and damaging actions that are taken by those who are insensitive to others. Aggressive people show little or no respect for others' basic human rights. They use their power to achieve results. They are not team players, unless they are playing games with their own ball. Aggressive people treat associates as expenses rather than as investments because they do not trust people.

Assertiveness Techniques

Since there are so many benefits to being assertive, it is to your advantage to learn a variety of ways to assert yourself. The more choices you have or techniques you know, and practice, the sooner you will become more assertive. Three techniques, for example, are:

◆ Mental Ai-Ki-Do

◆ Information Building

◆ Echoing

Mental Ai-Ki-Do

This technique can help you to accept criticism comfortably without becoming defensive.

Ai-Ki-Do is a martial art. Visualize a man holding up his hand in front of you. He asks that you hit this upheld hand with your fist. With all your force, you hit his hand. Since he did not move his hand when you hit it, he stops the forward motion of your swing.

5

Again you are asked to hit his hand with your fist. This time, in a split second before you're about to punch him, his fingers wrap around your fist. He then backs his hand away, while still holding on to yours, controlling the force you just threw. He accomplishes two things. First, by offering no resistance to your jab, he feels no pain. Second, by directing the momentum of your punch, he is in control of what's happening.

> **Don't fight negative feedback. Stay in control by deciding whether you agree with what was said.**

Use mental Ai-Ki-Do (control) when any negative feedback (mental fist) comes your way. Do not fight the feedback. Instead, accept the feedback by allowing it to come to you. Stay in control by deciding whether you agree to what was said. When you use your focused listening skills, try your best to stay even-tempered. Once you explode or hide, you start to lose control by giving in to the force.

Information Building

This technique will help you initiate and build relationships by sharing information about yourself.

One of the ways trust is built between associates is by the amount of knowledge that is shared by and about each other. Providing information about yourself first will encourage others to share their thoughts and feelings with you.

You do not have to discuss something of mutual interest. Nor should you restrict sharing information just because the other person has not disclosed much during your conversation. Remember, building relationships takes time.

Before meeting with someone, plan what kind of information would be appropriate to share. After sharing your thoughts and feelings, use humor and open-ended, nonleading questions to elicit feedback and to keep the conversation relaxed and flowing.

Depending upon how well you know the person and your own comfort level, start out with general information. Work up to sensitive, need-to-know information.

> One of the ways trust is built between associates is by the amount of knowledge that is shared by and about each other.

Echoing

This technique will strengthen your ability to say "no" respectfully without regrets. Use this technique only after exhausting these strategies:

◆ Inform whoever is requesting your services that you are unable to do the job if it does not fit into your priorities.

◆ Suggest a more suitable person to take on the assignment.

◆ If appropriate, offer some assistance or time to help with part of the project or task. Mention other possible ways to complete the work.

If these strategies do not work, and you are still being ordered or intimidated to handle a request, then use the echoing technique.

The technique is similar to an echo because you repeat what you desire. Stay composed and state over and over again what you want; in the process, you will teach others that you are serious and determined.

Stay composed and state over and over again what you want; in the process, you will teach others that you are serious and determined.

Some people feel this technique is a rude one because it requires you to be domineering. The technique certainly is used to get your way, but it should not be used exclusively. When it is inappropriate for you to budge on a certain point, the echoing technique will help you hold your ground with an associate, peer, supervisor, vendor, and even an irate and unreasonable customer.

Putting It All Together!

We've offered many suggestions throughout this book on how to manage conflict. But as we said in the beginning, it all comes down to you taking the responsibility for dealing with conflict—not avoiding it.

5

You have three choices with conflict situations—deal with them, ignore them, or leave the area of conflict. In most cases, the most prudent option is dealing with the conflict.

So just do it!

Self-Check: Chapter 5 Review

Anticipate two possible conflicts that you may face in the next few weeks. Using the form on the next page, describe how you would normally respond to these problems. Then put together a rough sketch of how you now intend to handle each situation. If you decide not to change the way you have dealt with the conflict, ask yourself why.

After conceptualizing the conflicts and your responses, use your Cause of Conflict Menu on page 35 to develop a more detailed and effective plan of action.

First Anticipated Conflict

Perceived Conflict	Normal Response	New Response

Second Anticipated Conflict

Perceived Conflict	Normal Response	New Response

5

Chapter 1
Chapter Review (page 18)

1. a. Be visionary.
   b. Give feedback.
   c. Get feedback.
   d. Define expectations.
   e. Review performance regularly.

2. a. Intellectual skills.
   b. Emotional skills.
   c. Interpersonal skills.
   d. Managerial skills.

3. True

4. Change

5. & 6. Answers will vary.

Chapter 2
Chapter Review (page 29)

1. I'd be glad to help. I'm very interested in listening to all of the possible strategies you thought of. Together, we should be able to come up with a good plan. Since I don't have the time to go over it now, could we meet at 4:00 today to discuss it?

2. I really don't know! It may have just been an oversight. Whatever it is, I'll check into it so we can get an answer.

3. Well, we're working extra hours lately, but so is she. Why don't we plan a meeting with her to find out why our work load has increased in the department?

Chapter 3
Take a Moment (page 47)

Both goals in the exercise on page 47 have identified who is responsible for accomplishing the goal and when the goal will be accomplished. But only the second goal states what result is expected (i.e., reduce delinquent accounts by 3 percent). Since the first goal does not state what is meant by acceptable orientations, it is not a valid goal. Goals must be measurable to avoid conflict.

Chapter Review (page 49)

Statements 1, 3, and 4 are true. Statements 2 and 5 are false.

6. Behaviors, aims, and methods

7. Intellectual, emotional, interpersonal, and managerial

8. Who will accomplish the goal?
   What is to be achieved?
   When will the goal be accomplished?

Chapter 4
Chapter Review (page 65)

1. a. Take responsibility.
   b. Uncover, define, and discuss.
   c. Ask and listen.
   d. Set goals and objectives.
   e. Follow up.

2. a. Listen with an open mind.
   b. Reassure the other person that you are interested.
   c. Offer positive feedback by paraphrasing what you've heard.

3. a. Everyone will be open and honest.
   b. Everyone will have a say and be heard.
   c. Everyone will listen to each other without argument or negative reaction and will keep a positive, caring attitude.
   d. Opinions and feelings must be supported by facts or examples of specific behavior.

5

Cause of Conflict Menu

Divergent views of conflict may exist in:

Behaviors

Intellectual
Planning: Conflict may surface because no time is spent to plan the training.

Emotional
Assertiveness: It seems neither man is being honest about why retraining is needed.

Interpersonal
Communication: No one is taking the responsibility to find a common understanding.

Managerial
Coaching: Frank is not giving the guidance Bill needs to ensure effective training.

Values
None: Although not obvious, values may differ because Frank wants Danny retrained so he does not lose another man in the department. He may look at people as expenses rather than as investments. If Bill's values differ, there will be conflict.

Aims

Missions, Objectives, Goals, Strategies, Values
Roles: No actual training goals, objectives, or standards have been stated. It is the lack of understanding of what is clearly expected from those involved (their roles) that often causes conflict to surface.

Methods

Strategies
None: Since no goals or objectives have been set, neither have any strategies.